Ballet for Martha
MAKING APPALACHIAN SPRING

Jan Greenberg and Sandra Jordan • Illustrated by Brian Floca

A NEAL PORTER BOOK   ROARING BROOK PRESS   NEW YORK

To Benjamin Avram who dances his way into my heart—J.G.

To my very good friend Nancy Arnold Goldstein—S.J.

To Timo, Sarah, Matilda, and Carl—B.F.

Text copyright © 2010 by Jan Greenberg and Sandra Jordan
Illustrations copyright © 2010 by Brian Floca
A Neal Porter Book
Published by Flash Point, an imprint of Roaring Brook Press
Roaring Brook Press is a division of Holtzbrinck Publishing Holdings Limited Partnership
175 Fifth Avenue, New York, New York 10010
www.roaringbrookpress.com

Distributed in Canada by H. B. Fenn and Company Ltd.

Cataloging-in-Publication Data is on file at the Library of Congress
ISBN: 978-1-59643-338-0

Roaring Brook Press books are availble for special promotions and premiums.
For details contact: Director of Special Markets, Holtzbrinck Publishers.

First Edition August 2010
Book design by Jennifer Browne
Printed in October 2010 in China by South China Printing Co. Ltd., Dongguan City, Guangdong Province
3 5 7 9 8 6 4 2

*S*ometimes art is made by one artist, working alone, but sometimes it is the result of artists working together—collaborating—to forge something new. It took more than a year and the imaginations of many talented people for Appalachian Spring, *the dance created by Martha Graham, to be performed on stage for the first time. The result was an American classic. This is the story of how it happened.*

The dancer and choreographer.
The composer.
The artist.
Together they created a ballet about a
new home, a new family, a new life.
A dance about America.

Martha Graham

Isamu Noguchi

Aaron Copland

Before it was a dance it was a story.

A story to be told in movement and
music, not in words,
a story of the frontier when pioneer
families traveled west to put down roots.
"A legend of American living,"
says Martha.

Martha asks the composer Aaron Copland
to create music for her ballet.
She writes a script for him, struggling to get
down on paper the rarin' to go rhythms
of a new land.
She waits for his answer.

"The characters are too severe," he tells Martha.
She adds Pocahontas and a runaway slave
to her tale. Then she cuts them out and
rewrites it again . . . and again.
"It took time to think it through."
At last Martha and Aaron agree.

The dance will take place in springtime, in the hills of western Pennsylvania, where a young farmer and his bride celebrate their wedding day.

There are no steps yet, but Aaron knows the way
Martha and her dancers move.
Her steps are unusual.
She moves differently from ballerinas.
No toe shoes. No tutus. No pirouettes.
"Nobody else seems anything like Martha," he says. "There's
something simple yet strong about her, which one thinks of
as very American."

"I wanted something more from dance," she says.
"Why should an arm, moved a certain way, suggest a
wildflower or a hand, or rain? The hand is too wonderful
a thing to be an imitation of something else."
She wants dance to be truth, truth about emotions.

"My dancers never fall to simply fall. They fall to rise."

contraction   release

The movements are not always pretty.
Not everyone likes Martha's new way of dancing.
Audiences have booed her performances,
but Martha never lets that stop her.

"Ugliness, if given a powerful voice, can be beautiful," she says.

Heretić, 1929

II

Aaron sits at the piano and tries out some notes.
As he searches for a melody,
he discovers an old song, a Shaker hymn.
*"It's a gift to be simple, it's a gift to be free,
it's a gift to come down where you want to be."*

The thread of the hymn winds through his music.
At the top of the score he writes "Ballet for Martha."
He records himself playing the finished piece
on a rickety, old piano and sends it to her.
This time he is the one waiting for an answer.

Martha listens to Aaron's music.
In it she hears the rollicking echo of a Virginia reel, the galloping
energy of a rodeo, the lilting melody of the Shaker hymn.
She begins work, turning steps into patterns that will bring
the dance to life.

There will be eight dancers in Martha's ballet.
Martha's role is the Bride.
Erick Hawkins, the man she loves, plays the Husbandman.
She bases the Pioneer Woman on her great-grandmother.
She went "from Virginia to Pennsylvania, her family in search of
good soil to till. . . . She was very beautiful and always very still."

Aaron's music suggests the movement,
fires the dancers' imaginations, dares them to do more.
Martha tells them to listen with their bodies.
Crouching on their knees, her dancers leap up,
using their stomach and leg muscles, breathing in and out.

If a movement doesn't work,
Martha tries it a different way.
And again a different way.
Nearly right is not enough.

Sometimes the dancers sit on the floor while she stands silently,
staring out the window.
"Let's try this," she says, turning.
She has a tantrum.
She screams.
She yells.
She throws a shoe.
The dancers wait. Martha always figures it out.

17

The music and the movement are two parts of the dance.
But a third part is needed.
She calls her friend, the artist Isamu Noguchi.

In his sculpture, Isamu carves marble, granite, or wood.
He transforms these materials into art.

When he works with Martha, he transforms an empty stage
into a fantastical world where the dancers can perform,
a world of painted poles, bronze stools, hanging ropes,
slanted steps, or a jungle gym.

He brings her models so small they fit into a matchbox.
If Martha says, "It is lovely, but I need to think about it,"
he snatches it away but always comes back with a new twist.
"I gave him the bones of an idea and he would return with
something whole."

Isamu's set is spare and angular, like Martha's way of dancing.
Peaked beams suggest a roofline.
A narrow skeleton of a rocking chair is the "woman's place,"
a special place Martha always asks him to design.

The set is just what Martha hoped for, "a new town,
a place where the first fence is going up."
"I blended, melded with her somehow, and we were one," says Isamu.

To the dancers the stage is like an obstacle course.
They dodge sharp angles and balance straight backed
on thin ledges. Even when the dancing is hard,
they must make it look easy.

Martha and her dancers tweak and polish,
practice and perfect.
Months later they are ready!
The troupe piles on a train for Washington, D.C.,
where the first performance will take place.

When Aaron arrives for the dress rehearsal,
he sees that the music he composed for one scene
has been used to go with another.
"It doesn't bother me a bit," he says,
"especially when it works."

"What will you call the ballet?" he asks.
"*Appalachian Spring*," says Martha.
She found these words in a poem
that has nothing to do with the ballet, she admits,
but she likes the sound of it.

As opening night grows near, the suspense mounts.
Will the world understand what they have done?

October 30, 1944. The audience gathers.

The music begins.
A piano,
four violins,
two violas,
two cellos,
a double bass,
a flute,
a clarinet,
and a bassoon.

One by one, the dancers walk onto the stage
to the solemn melody.

First the Preacher in his wide-brimmed hat.

The Pioneer Woman enters.

Next the Husbandman comes out.
As he walks, he touches the boards of their new farmhouse.
His dreams for the future are in that gesture.

Slowly the Bride glides in,
then runs to her groom.

28

The Preacher's four Followers file in.
The music turns lively and playful as the young girls dance in pairs,
then form circles, fluttering, skittering, reaching up to the sky.

29

The Pioneer Woman turns and sways, in and out and around them,
her steps light and graceful.
A quiet force of nature.

The bridegroom leaps and bounds like an acrobat, strutting, swaggering, showing off for his bride.

The Bride rocks an imaginary baby.

The Preacher joins the couple in marriage,
and the celebration begins.

The bridegroom twirls with his bride.
Then she prances in quick small steps.

35

The music turns fierce.
The Preacher delivers his fiery sermon.
Towering, glowering, leaping like a cat.
His long arms point toward the young couple.
Is he warning them about hard times ahead?
The Followers fall to their knees, rocking back and forth.

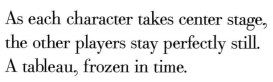

As each character takes center stage,
the other players stay perfectly still.
A tableau, frozen in time.

The ballet ends as the Husbandman and the
Bride enter their new house alone.
The final, lingering notes seem to ask,
"What will happen tomorrow?"

The audience rises, clapping.
The ballet is a triumph for the composer, the choreographer, and the artist.
Critics call the dance Martha's love letter, her valentine, her dance of hope.
Aaron wins prizes for his music.

But the life of *Appalachian Spring* goes on after that great night
to become an American favorite,
to be danced year after year.

New dancers will take their turns
to move to Aaron Copland's music,
to interpret Martha Graham's steps,
to dance through Isamu Noguchi's set.

42

And the collaboration
will be created anew.

Curtain Call

Martha Graham in Letter to the World, *photograph by Barbara Morgan, 1940.*

known for its modern approaches to dance. Eventually, she settled in Greenwich Village in New York, where she joined the Follies, with its wild assortment of animal acts and chorus girls, until she started her own dance troupe. There she invented a new style of dance based on emotion, breathing, and spare, angular forms. The Martha Graham Company struggled to survive, finally achieving worldwide fame. Martha—as everyone called her—performed until she was seventy-five but continued choreographing and teaching until her death in 1991. The Martha Graham Company was the first integrated dance company in the United States.

Martha Graham was sixteen when she saw her first dance performance. She had spotted a poster of the beautiful star and convinced her doting father to buy tickets. "He pinned a corsage of violets to my gray dress and that night my fate was sealed." Although her father, a respected physician, did not encourage Martha to become a dancer, he was a great influence on her life. Once he caught her in a lie and said he knew she wasn't telling the truth by the way she moved. "Movement doesn't lie," he told her, a remark she quoted all her life. Searching for truth through movement became her goal as a dancer.

The family had moved to California from Pennsylvania, where Martha was born in 1894. During the long train journey west, she watched the wide open landscape of America rolling by. This sense of never-ending space inspired *Appalachian Spring* and other dances she created (or choreographed) about America. In her early twenties, she studied and performed with the Denishawn company,

Aaron Copland by candlelight, studio in the Berkshires. September, 1946, photograph by Victor Kraft.

Aaron Copland, born in Brooklyn, New York, in 1900, was the son of Jewish immigrants from Russia. The family lived above their small department store, where Aaron and his four brothers and sisters grew up. Although he was the pampered baby of the family, his father was upset when he decided to be a musician. His older sister had taught him piano, as well as how to dance and drive a

44

car. She also convinced his parents to let him go to Paris at sixteen to study classical music composition. When he returned to the United States, he organized and produced concerts to showcase classical American music. As a composer, he was also influenced by American jazz and folk songs. He received many awards, including the Presidential Medal for Freedom and the Pulitzer Prize for *Appalachian Spring* in 1944. The following year, he rearranged the ballet score, which was for only thirteen instruments, for a fuller orchestra. It became one of his most popular works. In the 1950s, Copland, along with many other Americans, was unfairly accused of being disloyal to the United States in what was known as the McCarthy hearings. This outraged members of the music community, who said his patriotism was obvious in his music. The investigation was later dropped. Like Martha Graham, he looked to the big, open spaces of America for inspiration. Copland died in 1990, a respected musician who encouraged a whole new generation of American composers.

When Isamu Noguchi, born in Los Angeles in 1904, was three, he moved to Japan with his mother to meet his Japanese father, a well-known poet. Although his father had little to do with the young boy, his mother tried to teach him about Japanese culture, including practical skills, such as woodworking. Eventually she decided to send him to study in the United States to reclaim his American heritage. Thirteen-year-old Isamu, his suitcase packed with his carpenter tools, traveled alone by steamship to California, then by train to Indiana to a boarding school his mother had read about in a magazine. Like Martha, his first view of the huge American landscape was through a train window. He arrived at the school, only to find that it had closed to become an army base to train troops for World War I (1914–1918). Isamu stayed with a family in a nearby

Isamu Noguchi in his studio, photograph by Eliot Elisofon.

town until he graduated from a local high school. In college, he studied medicine before realizing his true interest in art. While he was struggling to establish himself as an artist in New York, he met Martha Graham, who asked him to design sets for *Frontier*, the first of more than twenty collaborations over more than forty years.

During World War II (1939–1945), with America at war with Japan and Germany, Noguchi volunteered to live in an internment camp with Japanese Americans who were being forcibly relocated from their homes. After the war, he opened sculpture studios in both Japan and the United States and spent much of his career traveling all over the world to create his artworks. In 1961, he established a studio in Long Island City, New York, that is now a museum showcasing his work. One of the world's most revered artists, Noguchi died in 1988.

Notes and Sources

BIBLIOGRAPHY

Acocella, Joan. *Twenty-eight Artists and Two Saints,
Essays.* New York: Pantheon, 2007.

Altshuler, Bruce. *Noguchi.* New York: Abbeville
Press, 1994.

Ashton, Dore. *Noguchi East and West.* New York:
Alfred A. Knopf, 1992.

Copland, Aaron and Vivian Perlis. *Copland: 1900
Through 1942.* New York: St. Martin's Marek, 1984.

Copland, Aaron and Vivian Perlis. *Copland:
Since 1943.* New York: St. Martin's Griffin, 1989.

deMille, Agnes. *Martha: The Life and Work of Martha Graham.* New York:
Random House, 1991.

Graham, Martha. *Blood Memory: An Autobiography.* New York: Doubleday, 1991.

Horosko, Marian. *Martha Graham: The Evolution of Her Dance Theory and
Training,* revised edition. Gainsville, FL: University Press of Florida, 2002.

Noguchi, Isamu. *A Sculptor's World.* New York: Harper and Row, 1968.

Noguchi, Isamu. *Essays and Conversations.* New York: Harrry N. Abrams, 1994.

Pollack, Howard. *Aaron Copland: The Life and Work of an Uncommon Man.*
Urbana, IL: University of Illinois Press, 1999.

Rychlak, Bonnie, Neil Printz, Janet Eilber. *Noguchi/Graham: Selected Works for
Dance, Essays.* New York: The Noguchi Foundation and Garden Museum,
2004.

Tracy, Robert. *Goddess: Martha Graham's Dancers Remember.* New York:
Limelight Editions, 1997.

Tracy, Robert. *Spaces of the Mind: Isamu Noguchi's Dance Designs.* New York:
Proscenium Publishers, 2001.

FILMS
A Dancer's World (1957), *Appalachian Spring* (1958), and *Night Journey*
(1961), Dance on Film, DVD, directed by Nathan Kroll (Criterion Collection,
2007).

WEB SITES
Martha Graham Center of Contemporary Dance
http://marthagraham.org/center

Noguchi Museum and Foundation
www.noguchi.org/museum&foundation.html

NOTES

Pg. 4   *A dance about America.* The collaboration between the three artists
began in 1942 as the United States entered World War II. Patriotic feelings were
running high. Philanthropist Elizabeth Sprague Coolidge gave a grant so that
Martha could commission three original ballet scores. One grant for $500 went
to Aaron Copland for what became *Appalachian Spring.*

Pg. 6   *"A legend of American living . . ."* Copeland II, 22.

Pg. 6   *"The characters are too severe . . ."* The first script Martha sent was
called "Daughter of Colchis" and included the characters of a fury and a muse.
When Copland didn't like it, she wrote a new script she called "House of
Victory." "It included . . . an Indian girl, and references to the Civil War."
"House of Victory" went back and forth several times, and finally included
eight parts, or scenes, and suggestions for musical themes including one that
asked for something that recalled a Shaker meeting or a gospel church. Graham, 226-232. Copland II, 30-48. Pollack, 388-404.

Pg. 6   *"It took time to think . . ."* Graham, 226.

Pg. 8   *"Nobody else seems anything like Martha . . . . And she's unquestionably
very American. There's something prim and restrained, simple yet strong about
her which one tends to think of as American."* Copeland II, 22.

Pg. 9   *"I wanted something more from dance."*
Graham, 108.

Pg. 9   *"My dancers never fall to simply fall. They
fall to rise."* Graham, 253.

Pg. 10   *"Ugliness, if given a powerful voice, can be
beautiful."* Graham, 134.

Pg. 13   *"It's a gift to be simple, it's a gift to be free,
it's a gift to come down where you want to be.
And when we find ourselves in the place just right
It will be the valley of love and delight,"*
Copland found the Shaker theme in a collection of
Shaker melodies compiled by Edward D. Andrews.

Pg. 13   The Shakers grew out of the Religious Society of Friends (Quakers)
in the late eighteenth century (1772). Their services included hymns such as
"Simple Gifts," work song, and ecstatic dancing (from which they derived
the name Shakers). Once Shakers had thousands of followers and eighteen
communities in the United States. As of 2006, there are four living Shakers.

Pg. 15   *"from Virginia to Pennsylvania . . ."* Graham, 232.

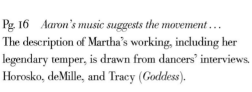

Pg. 16   *Aaron's music suggests the movement . . .*
The description of Martha's working, including her
legendary temper, is drawn from dancers' interviews.
Horosko, deMille, and Tracy (*Goddess*).

Pg. 16   [Martha] dares them to do more: "That's
the great thing about Aaron's music for dance—it
drives the choreographer. It drives the dancer."
Pearl Lang, who danced one of the four Followers, Copeland II, 43.

Pg. 16   *Martha tells them to listen with their bodies.* Graham, 253.

Pg. 18   "Dancing in Noguchi sets, you felt you were in a world that the great
sculptor had created, a whole new world, one that was not on a stage." Erick
Hawkins in Tracy (*Goddess*), 44.

Pg. 18   *"It is lovely, but I need to think about it."* Graham, 222.

Pg. 18   *"I gave him the bones of an idea . . ."* Graham, 218.

Pg. 19   *A narrow skeleton of a rocking chair . . .* Tracy (*Spaces*), 44.

Pg. 19   *"I blended, melded with her . . ."* Noguchi (*Essays*), 121.

Pg. 20   Janet Eilber, formerly a dancer with the Martha Graham Company
and now their artistic director, wrote "A Dancer Speaks Out: The Untold
Story of the Noguchi Sets," Rychlak, 59.

Pg. 20   The title for the ballet, *Appalachian Spring*, is taken from "The
Bridge," a poem by Hart Crane. The poem had nothing to do with Martha's
dance or Copland's music, but as she said, she liked the sound of it. Copland
said he laughed when people told him they could hear the coming of spring in
his music. He wasn't thinking of that when he wrote it, but what they heard
was up to them. Graham, 230–31; Pollack, 402.

Pg. 22   *Appalachian Spring* premiered at Coolidge Auditorium at the Library
of Congress in Washington, D.C., October 30, 1944, as part of a three-day gala
to honor Elizabeth Sprague Coolidge's eightieth birthday. Martha's friend and
longtime musical director Louis Horst conducted.

Pg. 24   *One by one, the dancers walk
onto the stage:* Erick Hawkins,
Martha's husband as well as the
first male dancer in her company,

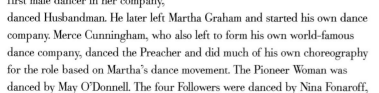

danced Husbandman. He later left Martha Graham and started his own dance
company. Merce Cunningham, who also left to form his own world-famous
dance company, danced the Preacher and did much of his own choreography
for the role based on Martha's dance movement. The Pioneer Woman was
danced by May O'Donnell. The four Followers were danced by Nina Fonaroff,
Marjorie Mazia, Yuriko, and Pearl Lang.

Pg. 36   *The Preacher delivers his fiery sermon.* Merce Cunningham was a very
intense dancer, and the way he performed the Preacher reflected that. In a gala
performance in 1987, conducted by Aaron Copland, Mikhail Baryshnikov
danced the Husbandman and Rudolph Nureyev danced the Preacher. Nureyev
saw the Preacher as a comic figure, and that's the way he danced it.

Pg. 44   *"He pinned a corsage of violets to my gray dress . . ."* Graham, 56.

PHOTOGRAPHS

The authors gratefully acknowledge the permission granted to reproduce the
copyrighted material in this book. Every effort has been made to obtain
permission for the use of this material.

Martha Graham in *Letter to the World*. 1940 © Barbara Morgan, The Barbara
Morgan Archives/Jerome Robbins Dance Division, New York Public Library for
the Performing Arts, Astor, Lenox, and Tilden Foundations.

Aaron Copland by candlelight, studio in the Berkshires. September, 1946 ©
Victor Kraft, Aaron Copland Archive at the Library of Congress.

Isamu Noguchi in his studio 1946 © Eliot Elisofon, The Isamu Noguchi
Foundation and Garden Museum/Photography Collection, Harry Ransom
Humanities Research Center, The University of Texas at Austin.

Isamu Noguchi, stage set of *Appalachian Spring* © 2009, The Isamu Nogushi
Foundation and Garden Museum, New York/Artists Rights Society (ARS),
New York.

Martha Graham and Erick Hawkins in Appalachian Spring, *set by Isamu Noguchi, 1944.*

ACKNOWLEDGMENTS

This project was truly a collaboration, not only between the authors and illustrator, but also with the many people who gave so generously of their time to answer questions, give advice, offer opinions and insights, and provide support for this book: Janet Eilber, the elegant artistic director of Martha Graham Dance Company; Denise Vale, senior associate of the Martha Graham Dance Company, and all the many talented members of the Martha Graham Dance Company; David Robertson, music director, St. Louis Symphony; and David Halen, concertmaster, St. Louis Symphony, for their thoughtful insights into Aaron Copland's music; Yuriko, dancer, teacher and choreographer, who danced one of the Followers in the original production of *Appalachian Spring*;

Mimi Arsham for her memories of Martha Graham and the making of the video of *Appalachian Spring*; Marcus Shulkind, Dick Jackson, Sybille Jagusch at the Library of Congress for a look inside and backstage at the auditorium where *Appalachian Spring* was first performed; Heidi Coleman, photo archivist at the Noguchi Foundation and Garden Museum; Aaron Copland Collection at the Library of Congress; Jan and Sandra's stalwart agent George Nicholson; our brilliant editor, creative advisor, and friend, Neal Porter; talented designer and blithe spirit, Jennifer Browne; assistant and permissions sleuth, David Langva; managing editor and the calmer of all troubled waters, Jill Freshney; and the miracle worker who oversees production, Susan Doran.